Why Why Why were Vikings so fierce?

First published as hardback in 2006 by
Miles Kelly Publishing Ltd, Bardfield Centre,
Great Bardfield, Essex, CM7 4SLCopyright © Miles
Kelly Publishing Ltd 2006

This 2009 edition published and distributed by:

Mason Crest Publishers Inc.
370 Reed Road, Broomall, Pennsylvania 19008
(866) MCP-BOOK (toll free)
www.masoncrest.com

Why Why Why—
Were Vikings So Fierce?
ISBN 978-1-4222-1591-3
Library of Congress Cataloging-in-Publication data
is available

Why Why Why—?
Complete 23 Title Series
ISBN 978-1-4222-1568-5

Printed in the United States of America

Contents

Where did Vikings come from?   4

Who discovered Greenland?   5

Why did Vikings carry boats?   5

Which king killed his brother?   6

Who tried to stop the waves?   7

What was the jelling stone?   7

What was a dragon ship?   8

Did Vikings have maps?   8

Who was afraid of the Vikings?   9

Why were Vikings so fierce?   10

Did swords have names?   10

What weapons did Vikings use?   11

Who rode an eight-legged horse? 12

Who controlled the thunder? 13

Why were warriors so brave? 13

Why did animals live in houses? 14

What were runes? 15

Why did Vikings get ill? 15

How did grass provide food? 16

Did Vikings have factories? 17

Why was the sea so important? 17

What was sold at markets? 18

Who were the Vikings scared of? 19

How were quarrels settled? 19

Did girls go to school? 20

Were wives expensive? 21

Who used wooden swords? 21

What did people wear? 22

Did people wear jewelry? 23

Did Vikings wear make up? 23

How did people get clean? 24

Did Vikings have toilets? 24

How did Vikings wear their hair? 25

How did Vikings prepare for battle? 26

What was a saga? 27

What did people do for fun? 27

Who defeated the Vikings? 28

How do we remember the Vikings? 29

Was Santa a Viking? 29

Quiz time 30

Index 32

Where did Vikings come from?

The Vikings lived about 2000 years ago. Viking warriors came from Denmark, Sweden and Norway to raid villages and steal treasure. Viking families began to settle in England, Ireland, Scotland and France. They explored Iceland, Greenland and Russia — and even traveled as far as North America.

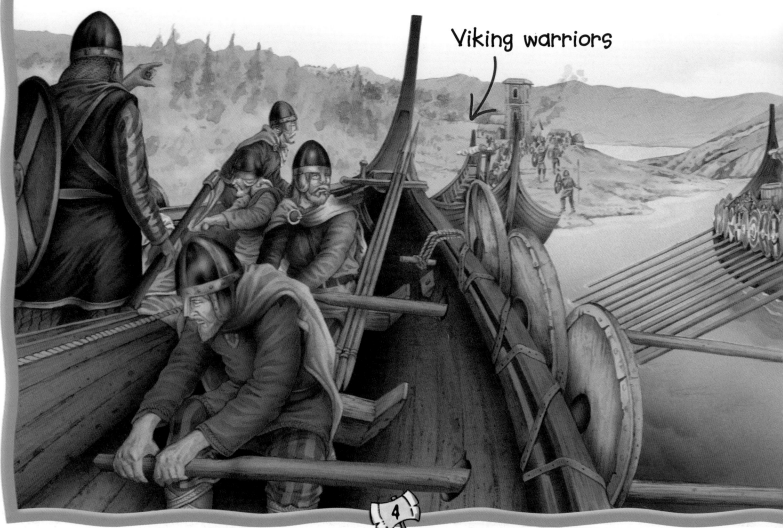

Viking warriors

Who discovered Greenland?

A Viking called Erik the Red discovered Greenland. It was a dark and icy place but Erik wanted people to come and live there. He called it 'Greenland' so they would think it was a warm place full of trees and grass.

Greenland

Why did Vikings carry their boats?

In winter, Vikings made long overland journeys. In some places, they carried their boats over ground between rivers. The Vikings were brave adventurers, keen to seek new land and treasures. Each journey took several years.

Imagine

Can you imagine discovering a new country? What would you call it?

Pirates!

The word 'Viking' means 'pirates,' 'port-attackers,' or 'people of the bays.' This tells us that Vikings spent their lives close to the sea.

Which king killed his brother?

When a Viking king died, each of his sons had an equal right to his throne. Erik Bloodaxe was famous for his cruelty. He wanted to be king so much, he killed both of his brothers and became King Erik of Norway.

Think

What would your Viking name be? You can make it as funny as you like!

Erik Bloodaxe

My name is...!

Many Viking rulers had strange names such as Svein Forkbeard, Einar Falsemouth, Magnus Barelegs, and Thorfinn Skullsplitter!

King Cnut →

Who tried to stop the waves?

King Cnut was a Viking king of Denmark, Norway and England. He was a cruel ruler. However, Cnut said he was a good Christian. To prove it, he ordered the waves to stop. When they did not he said, "This proves that I am weak. Only God can control the sea."

What was the Jelling Stone?

King Harald Bluetooth built a church at Jelling, in Denmark. Outside the church was a memorial for his dead parents. It was called the Jelling Stone and was decorated with Viking and Christian carvings.

What was a dragon ship?

Vikings built ships called 'drakar,' or dragon ships. These ships were designed for war. They were long, speedy and beautifully carved. Because they were so light, they could sail easily onto beaches.

Drakar ship

Did Vikings have maps?

No, they didn't. The Vikings used the positions of the Sun, Moon and stars to guide them on their travels. They also followed the direction the wind was blowing in.

Remember

Can you remember the Viking word for 'dragon ship?'

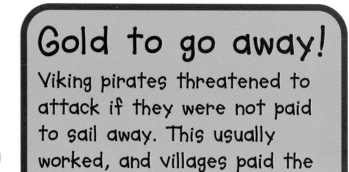

Gold to go away!

Viking pirates threatened to attack if they were not paid to sail away. This usually worked, and villages paid the gold – again and again!

Who was afraid of the Vikings?

Vikings could be very scary! People living in seaside villages were often afraid of them. Gangs of warriors carried out raids on defenseless villages. They stole valuable treasure and healthy young men and women to sell as slaves.

Viking raid →

Why were Vikings so fierce?

To scare their enemies in battle! Viking warriors dressed in animal skins and charged at their enemies, howling and growling like wolves, and chewing at their shields. These warriors were called berserkirs and this is where the word 'berserk' comes from.

Berserkir

Did swords have names?

Viking warriors loved their swords so much, they even gave them names such as 'Sharp Biter'! When a warrior died, he would be buried with his sword by his side.

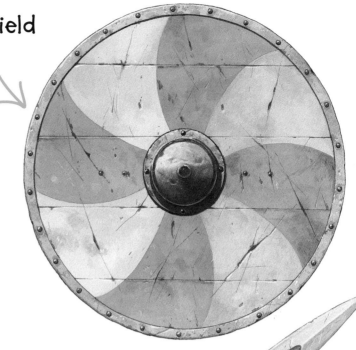
Shield

Design

Draw your own Viking sword and shield. What name would you give to your sword?

What weapons did Vikings use?

Vikings had to make or buy all of their weapons. Poor soldiers carried knives and spears. Wealthy Vikings had metal helmets and tunics, and fine, sharp swords. They carried a round shield that was made of wood covered with leather.

Sword

Helmet

Soldier women!

Women went to war but they did not fight. Instead, they nursed wounded warriors and cooked meals for hungry soldiers.

Who rode an eight-legged horse?

Odin

Odin was king of the Viking gods. He rode an eight-legged horse called Sleipnir and had two ravens called Thought and Memory. Odin sat on a high throne so he could see all of the Universe. Sometimes he liked to dress as a traveler and take a holiday in the human world.

Discover

Can you find out about any other Viking gods or goddesses – which one is your favorite?

Who controlled the thunder?

The storm god Thor controlled thunder. Viking farmers hated thunderstorms because they ruined their crops. They would pray to Thor to stop the thunder and let their crops grow. Thor rode in his chariot through the clouds holding a giant hammer and thunderbolt.

Thor

Sea god!
Njord was the god of the sea. He was married to the giantess Skadi, who watched over the mountains.

Why were warriors so brave?

Because they believed they would go to heaven when they died. Vikings thought that dead warriors were remembered forever, and that they went to heaven to feast with the gods.

Why did animals live in houses?

Homes were needed to shelter animals, as well as people. In towns, pigs, goats and horses were kept in sheds. In the countryside, the weather could be cold and wet. Farmers lived in longhouses, with an area for animals at one end. This meant that the people and animals stayed warm and dry.

Longhouse

Room for the animals

What were runes?

Runes were the 16 letters of the Viking alphabet. People used them for labeling belongings with the owner's name, recording accounts, keeping calendars and sending messages. There was no paper, so runes were carved onto wood.

← Runes

Make

With a cardboard box, make your own Viking house. You could even glue some grass to the roof.

Why did Vikings get ill?

Vikings suffered from chest diseases. This was because their houses did not have windows and were often damp and full of smoke from the fire burning on the stove.

Grass roof

Outside toilet

Precious cow!

Viking farmers loved cows! A cow was precious because it gave milk, clothing and meat, and its droppings were spread on the fields to help crops grow.

How did grass provide food?

Grassy fields provided food for animals and people. Sheep and cows needed fresh grass to eat. These animals then provided milk and meat for people to eat. Farmers also cut the grass and dried it out to make hay to feed the animals in the winter.

Farm

Discover

Have a look at the labels inside your clothes. What are your clothes made of?

Did Vikings have factories?

No! Vikings had no machines, so all work was done by hand. Families had to make or grow everything they needed. They built their own houses and furniture and they made their own clothes and toys. Blacksmiths made weapons and tools for people to work with.

Blacksmiths

Why was the sea so important?

Because people could catch fish to eat. People also gathered shellfish from the seashore for dinner. Vikings built their villages close to the sea in case they needed to travel to new places.

Itchy clothes!

Clothes were made of wool and could be very itchy. Women made smoother, finer cloth to wear as underwear.

What was sold at markets?

Vikings held markets on the beach. Farmers would sell meat, milk and fur to travellers. Some Vikings travelled a long way to buy different things to sell. They would buy woollen cloth from Britain, wine from France, glass from Germany, jewelry from Russia and spices from the Middle East.

Market

How were quarrels settled?

Many quarrels were settled by fighting. Quarrels between families could continue for months. This lead to people on both sides being killed, until each family was prepared to seek peace.

Settling an argument

Bone comb!

Animal bones that were left over from mealtimes were used to carve combs, beads and pins. Deer antlers were used to make finer combs.

Pretend

With a friend, pretend to be a pirate and Viking. Who is more scared of who?

Who were the Vikings scared of?

Pirates from Russia! They sailed across the sea to steal treasure from Viking towns. So Vikings defended their towns with wooden walls and troops of warriors.

Did girls go to school?

No, they didn't. Instead of going to school, girls helped their mothers with cooking and cleaning, fed farm animals, fetched water, gathered wood, nuts and berries and learned how to spin, weave and sew.

Viking girls

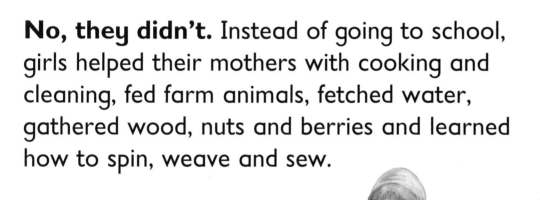

Think
Can you think why it was important for young boys to practice fighting with wooden swords?

Were wives expensive?

If a Viking man wanted to marry, he had to ask the woman's father for permission and pay him a bride price. If the father accepted this, the marriage went ahead, even if the woman did not agree.

Who used wooden swords?

Viking boys practiced fighting with wooden swords and small, lightweight shields. They also learned how to ride horses and use real weapons. They had to be ready to fight by the time they were 15 or 16 years old.

Viking boys

Wise women!

Many young women died having a baby. This meant there were fewer older women. Older women were thought to be very wise and people respected them for their knowledge and experience.

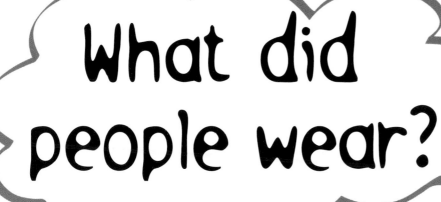

What did people wear?

Vikings wore lots of layers to keep out the cold. Women wore long dresses of linen or wool with a woollen over-dress. Men dressed in wool tunics over linen shirts and woollen trousers. Men also wore fur or sheepskin caps while women wore headscarves and shawls.

Clothing

Dress up

Have a look through your wardrobe and see if you can dress up as a Viking!

Did people wear jewelry?

Both men and women liked to wear lots of jewelry. They thought it made them look good and it also showed how rich they were. Rings and arm braclets were given to warriors as rewards for fighting bravely in battle.

Gold ring

Necklace

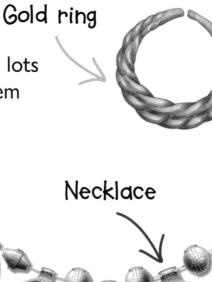

Brooch

Did Vikings wear make up?

Viking men wore make-up! They particularly liked to wear make up around their eyes – probably made from soot or crushed berries. They thought it made them look more handsome.

23

How did people get clean?

Vikings bathed by pouring water over red-hot stones to create clouds of steam. They sat in the steam to make themselves sweat, then rubbed their skin with birch twigs to help loosen the dirt. Then they jumped into a pool of cold water to rinse off.

Keeping clean

Did Vikings have toilets?

Yes they did. Houses had an outside toilet that was simply a bucket, or a hole in the ground with a wooden seat on top. Panels of woven twigs were set up around the toilet. Dried moss or grass was used as toilet paper.

Sloping house!

Longhouses were built on a slope. Then waste from the animals ran downhill – away from people living inside!

Hairstyles

How did Vikings wear their hair?

Men let their fringes grow long, and braided the strands that hung down either side of their face. Women also kept their hair long. They left it flowing loose until they married, then tied it in a beautiful knot at the nape of their neck.

Try

Is your hair long enough to braid like a Viking? Ask an adult to help you.

How did Vikings prepare for battle?

Viking sports were good training for war. Spear-throwing, sword-fighting and archery – shooting at targets with bows and arrows – were all popular. They helped boys and young men to become fit and strong and prepared them for using weapons.

Archer →

Drinking horns

Vikings liked to drink ale from cups carved from cattle horns. Warriors would carry these drinking horns on their long journeys.

What was a saga?

A saga was a story that Vikings told to honor heroes who died in battle. The sagas were told to ensure that heroes' names and fame never died. These stories were passed on by word of mouth for many years.

Saga

What did people do for fun?

Vikings liked music and dancing. Kings would hire dancers, clowns, jugglers and singers to entertain their guests at feasts. Vikings also enjoyed playing practical jokes and listening to stories about gods and heroes.

Write
What is your favorite story? Maybe you could try and write one of your own.

Who defeated the Vikings?

Kings of England, Scotland and Wales defeated the Vikings. In 1014, King Brian Boru drove the Vikings from Ireland, and Viking rule ended in England in 1042. Viking kings still ruled parts of Scotland until 1266.

Viking defeat

Festival

How do we remember the Vikings?

Today, people still celebrate Viking festivals. In the Shetland Isles, people dress up as Vikings then burn a lifesize model of a Viking warship. They do this to remember the Viking festival of Yule, held every January.

Was Santa a Viking?

Santa was a Viking god! Yule (mid-winter) was an important Viking festival. Vikings held feasts and exchanged gifts. They also believed that Viking gods travelled across the sky, bringing good things — just like Santa!

Do you speak Viking?

Many Viking words for everyday things still survive such as 'sister,' 'knife' and 'egg.'

Quiz time

Do you remember what you have read about the Vikings? These questions will test your memory. The pictures will help you. If you get stuck, read the pages again.

page 5

1. Why did Vikings carry their boats?

2. Which king killed his brother?

page 6

3. Who was afraid of the Vikings?

page 9

4. Did swords have names?

page 10

5. Who controlled the thunder?

page 13

6. Why did animals live in houses?

page 14

7. Why was the sea so important?

page 17

page 24

11. Did Vikings have toilets?

8. Who used wooden swords?

page 21

12. Who defeated the Vikings?

page 28

9. Were wives expensive?

page 21

page 29

13. Was Santa a Viking?

10. How did people get clean?

page 24

Answers

1. To transport them between rivers
2. Erik Bloodaxe
3. People living in seaside villages
4. Viking warriors gave their swords names
5. Thor, the storm god
6. To keep them warm and dry
7. So people could catch fish to eat
8. Viking boys
9. Viking men had to pay money to their bride's father
10. They steamed themselves
11. Yes, they did
12. Kings of England, Scotland and Wales
13. Yes, Santa was a Viking god

31

Index

A
ale 26
alphabet 15
animals 20
  bones 19
  food 16
  in houses 14, 25
antlers 19
archery 26

B
bathing 24–25
beads 23
berserkirs 10
blacksmiths 17
boats 5, 8–9, 29
bones 19
bows and arrows 26
boys 21, 26
Brian Boru, King 28
brides 21

C
carvings 7
cattle horns 26
Christianity 7
churches 7
clothes 10, 17, 22
Cnut, King 7
combs 19
cows 15, 16, 26

D
dancing 27
Denmark 4, 7
dragon ships 8–9

dresses 22
drinking horns 26

E
Einar Falsemouth 7
England 4, 7, 28
Erik Bloodaxe, King 6
Erik the Red 5

F
farmers
  animals 15, 16
  longhouses 14
  markets 18
  thunderstorms 13
feasts 27, 29
festivals 29
fighting 19, 21, 26
fish 17
food
  for animals 16
  fish 17
  markets 18
  meat 16, 18
  milk 16, 18
France 4, 18
furniture 17
furs 10, 18, 22

G
Germany 18, 23
girls 20
glass beads 23
gods and goddesses
    12–13, 27, 29
gold 9, 23
grass 16
Greenland 4, 5

H
hairstyles 25
Harald Bluetooth, King
    7
hay 16

heaven 13
helmets 11
heroes 27
horns, drinking from 26
horses 12–13, 21
houses 14–15, 17, 25

I
Iceland 4
illness 15
Ireland 4, 28

J, K
Jelling Stone 7
jewelry 23
kings 6, 27, 28

L
linen 22
longhouses 14, 25

M
Magnus Barelegs 7
make-up 23
maps 8
markets 18
marriage 21, 25
meat 16, 18
Middle East 18
milk 16, 18
music 27

N
names 7, 10
Njord 13
North America 4
Norway 4, 6, 7

O, P, Q
Odin 12
pirates 5, 9, 19
quarrels 19

R
raids 9
runes 15
Russia 4, 18, 19

S
sagas 27

Santa 29
school 20
Scotland 4, 28
sea 7, 17, 19
sheep 16
shellfish 17
Shetland Islands 29
shields 10, 11, 21
ships 5, 8–9, 29
shirts 22
Skadi 13
slaves 9
spears 26
sports 26
steam baths 24–25
stones, carved 7
stories 27
Svein Forkbeard 7
Sweden 4
swords 10, 11, 21, 26

T
Thor 13
Thorfinn Skullsplitter 7
thunderstorms 13
toilets 15, 24
tools 17
towns 19
toys 17
treasure 4, 5, 9, 19
trousers 22
tunics 22

V
villages 17

W, Y
Wales 28
warriors 4, 9, 10, 13
weapons 11, 17, 21, 26
women
  clothes 22
  hairstyles 25
  marriage 21, 25
  older women 21
  at war 11
wool 17, 18, 22
words 29
Yule 29